ANCIENT ROME INSIDE OUT

John Malam

Crabtree Publishing Company
www.crabtreebooks.com

ANCIENT WORLDS INSIDE OUT

Author: John Malam

Editors: Sarah Eason, Kelly Spence, Ellen Rodger, and Kathy Middleton

Editorial director: Kathy Middleton

Design: Paul Myerscough

Cover design: Paul Myerscough

Photo research: Rachel Blount

Proofreader: Wendy Scavuzzo

Production coordinator and Prepress technician: Tammy McGarr

Print coordinator: Margaret Amy Salter

Consultant: John Malam, archaeologist

Written and produced for Crabtree Publishing Company by Calcium Creative

Front Cover

BKGD: The Colosseum in Rome, an oval amphitheater in which 50,000 to 80,000 spectators could watch gladiator combat.
Inset: Helmet with visor for combat in the gladiator arena.

Title page

BKGD: The Appian Way, a very long ancient Roman road built to transport troops from Rome to the port of Brindisi in the south of Italy.
Inset: An honorary statue of an emperor for a public space. The head was replaced during an 18th-century restoration to feature Emperor Domitian who reigned from 81 to 96 CE.

Photo Credits:

t=Top, bl=Bottom Left, br=Bottom Right

Dreamstime: Joserpizarro: p. 13b; Getty Images: DEA/G. DAGLI ORTI/De Agostini: p. 15b; The Paul J. Getty Museum: Digital image courtesy of the Getty's Open Content Program: p. 28b; Shutterstock: AOF_SNIPER: p. 28–29bg; Tony Baggett: p. 24–25; Rudy Balasko: p. 4–5; Roxana Bashyrova: p. 14–15; BlackMac: p. 10–11; Mark Godden: p. 22–23; Iakov Kalinin: p. 6–7; K3S: p. 26–27; Luciano Mortula: p. 18–19; Nejron Photo: p. 16–17; Lefteris Papaulakis: p. 23t; Jaime Pharr: p. 20–21; Jannis Tobias Werner: pp. 1bg, 12–13; Vladimir Wrangel: p. 27t; The Walters Art Museum: Museum purchase, 1990: p. 25b; Museum purchase with funds provided by the S. & A.P. Fund, 1969: pp. 1fg, 11r; Wikimedia Commons: CristianChirita : p. 21t; Jean-Pol Grandmont: p. 19r; Carole Raddato from Frankfurt, Germany: pp. 3, 8–9, 17t.

Map p. 5 by Geoff Ward. Artwork p. 29 by Venetia Dean.

Cover: Shutterstock: Studio Barcelona (bg); Wikimedia Commons: Carole Raddato from Frankfurt, Germany (br)

Library and Archives Canada Cataloguing in Publication

Malam, John, author
    Ancient Rome inside out / John Malam.

(Ancient worlds inside out)
Includes index.
Issued in print and electronic formats.
ISBN 978-0-7787-2882-5 (hardcover).--
ISBN 978-0-7787-2896-2 (softcover).--
ISBN 978-1-4271-1850-9 (HTML)

    1. Rome--Social life and customs--Juvenile literature.
2. Rome--Civilization--Juvenile literature. 3. Rome--Antiquities-
-Juvenile literature. 4. Material culture--Rome--Juvenile
literature. 5. Rome--History--Juvenile literature. I. Title.

DG77.M29 2017   j937   C2016-907265-7
                                     C2016-907266-5

Library of Congress Cataloging-in-Publication Data

Names: Malam, John, 1957- author.
Title: Ancient Rome inside out / John Malam.
Description: New York : Crabtree Publishing Company, [2017] |
  Series: Ancient worlds inside out | Includes index.
Identifiers: LCCN 2017000080 (print) | LCCN 2017000888 (ebook) |
  ISBN 9780778728825 (library binding : alk. paper) |
  ISBN 9780778728962 (pbk. : alk. paper) |
  ISBN 9781427118509 (Electronic HTML)
Subjects: LCSH: Rome--Civilization--Juvenile literature. |
  Rome--History--Juvenile literature.
Classification: LCC DG77 .M319 2017 (print) | LCC DG77 (ebook) |
  DDC 937--dc23
LC record available at https://lccn.loc.gov/2017000080

Crabtree Publishing Company

www.crabtreebooks.com   1-800-387-7650

Printed in Canada/032017/EF20170202

Published in Canada
Crabtree Publishing
616 Welland Ave.
St. Catharines, Ontario
L2M 5V6

Published in the United States
Crabtree Publishing
PMB 59051
350 Fifth Avenue, 59th Floor
New York, New York 10118

Published in the United Kingdom
Crabtree Publishing
Maritime House
Basin Road North, Hove
BN41 1WR

Published in Australia
Crabtree Publishing
3 Charles Street
Coburg North
VIC, 3058

CONTENTS

WHO WERE THE ANCIENT ROMANS?

Italy is a country in southern Europe. It was home to the Romans, one of the greatest ancient civilizations. Roman civilization spread over 500 years to include an empire that stretched east to western Asia, and west to Britain.

Rise of the Romans

Many different groups of people lived in Italy before the Romans. One group, the Latins, lived in villages in central Italy on seven low hills close to the Tiber River. These farming villages developed into the city of Rome, whose **citizens** were known as Romans. At first, a **rival** group from the north, called the Etruscans, ruled over the city. In 509 B.C.E., the Roman people **overthrew** the Etruscan kings and took control. Rome then became a **republic**. It was ruled by the Senate, which was a **political** body or council made up of leading Roman citizens. As the Romans grew in power, they took over all of Italy. They then spread out from Italy and took control of nearby lands.

Emperors and the Roman Empire

In 27 B.C.E., during a time of confusion and **crisis**, Roman **noble** and general Octavian seized power. The Senate gave him the name Augustus, which means "deeply respected one." The Roman people called him *imperator*, from which we get the word "**emperor**." Augustus was the first Roman emperor. He expanded the Roman Empire. Many emperors (about 80 in 500 years) followed after Augustus's death, and the empire reached the height of its power in 117 C.E. The Romans controlled much of western and central Europe, the Middle East, and North Africa. About 50 million people came under Roman control.

Decline and Fall of the Roman Empire

The borders of the vast empire were not secure, and enemy tribes invaded. In 284 C.E., the Romans divided the empire into Western and Eastern parts, hoping smaller parts would be easier to control. But, in 410 C.E., Rome was taken over by an invading tribe, and in 476 C.E. the last emperor of the Western Empire **abdicated**.

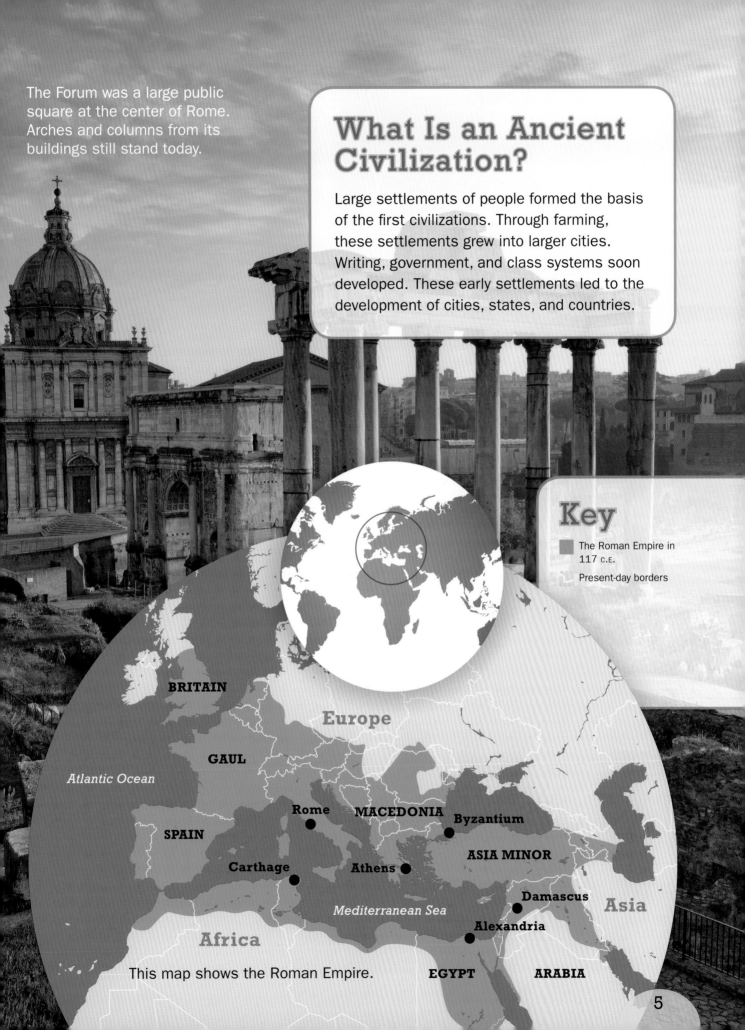

The Forum was a large public square at the center of Rome. Arches and columns from its buildings still stand today.

What Is an Ancient Civilization?

Large settlements of people formed the basis of the first civilizations. Through farming, these settlements grew into larger cities. Writing, government, and class systems soon developed. These early settlements led to the development of cities, states, and countries.

Key

■ The Roman Empire in 117 c.e.

□ Present-day borders

BRITAIN

Europe

GAUL

Atlantic Ocean

SPAIN

Rome   MACEDONIA   Byzantium

ASIA MINOR

Carthage   Athens

Damascus   Asia

Mediterranean Sea

Alexandria

Africa

This map shows the Roman Empire.   EGYPT   ARABIA

DIGGING UP THE PAST

The ancient Romans had their own mythology, or collection of stories. Many of these myths were about ordinary people, or the powerful gods and goddesses who ruled daily life. One of the best known Roman myths was the story of Romulus and Remus, and how Rome began. The more Romans told it, the more they believed it.

The Wolf and the Twins

Twin boys Romulus and Remus were said to be the sons of Mars, the god of war, and the human daughter of a king. The twins' great-uncle overthrew their grandfather and took his crown. He feared the boys would become powerful and take it back. So he threw them into the Tiber River. Their basket was found by a she-wolf, who looked after them and fed them with her own milk. Later, a shepherd raised the boys as his own sons. When Romulus and Remus grew up and learned what their great-uncle had done, they killed him in revenge. They decided to build a city at the place where they had been thrown into the river. They argued about which of them should be king and what to call the city. In his rage, Romulus killed Remus. He built the city on his own, and named it Rome, after himself. The Romans said this happened on April 21, 753 B.C.E. Every year, on April 21, they celebrated Rome's birthday with a festival.

The True Origins of Rome

Today's **archaeologists** have discovered evidence of Rome's true origins, buried deep beneath the modern city. They have found that Rome began around 1000 B.C.E. as a cluster of small villages. By around 750 B.C.E., the villages had joined together to form a town.

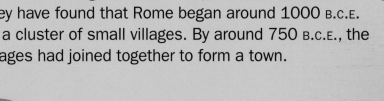

The city of Rome grew up along the banks of the Tiber River, shown here in modern times. The bridge in the foreground is the Sant'Angelo Bridge. It was completed in 135 B.C.E. by Roman emperor Hadrian.

What Are Primary Sources?

Archaeology is the study of how people lived in the past. Archaeologists learn about how and where people lived through the materials they left behind. These materials are called **primary sources**. They were made during a specific period of time, and include **artifacts** and written documents. Examining primary sources provides a window into how people lived long ago. Archaeologists **analyze** primary sources to **interpret** their meanings.

ROME, CAPITAL OF THE WORLD

The Romans were incredibly proud of Rome, which they described in their language as *caput mundi*, meaning "capital of the world." The city was at its grandest around 300 C.E., when about 1.5 million people lived there.

Rome at Its Peak

We have a good idea how Rome looked around 300 C.E. Some of its buildings still stand today, and ancient Roman **surveyors** made a list of the city's buildings. According to the list, Rome had 28 libraries, 1,352 fountains for drinking water, 254 mills for producing bread flour, and 46,602 apartments and small houses. The city also had 11 large and 856 small public bathhouses. Bathhouses were where people bathed together and discussed business.

Houses and Apartments

Rome was a city of contrasts. While the rich lived in large private houses, the poor lived in cramped apartment blocks. The house of a wealthy family was a low-rise building, with the dining room, servants' quarters, kitchen, bedrooms, and storerooms laid out around an open-air courtyard in the center of the building. Rooms were heated by warm air that circulated under the floors and inside the walls. The poor, who formed the bulk of Rome's population, lived in one-room apartments, in blocks that were up to five stories tall. Families lived in rooms that were small, dark, cold, and dirty. They did not have running water, heating, or toilets.

History Up Close

The city of Rome had a network of about 56 miles (90 km) of roads, streets, and alleys. It could not have been easy for people to find their way around. So, in the 200s C.E., a street map known as the *Forma Urbis* was attached to the outside of a building. Carved onto 150 **marble** slabs, the map measured 60 feet by 45 feet (18 m by 14 m). It showed every street, building, store, house, room, and staircase in Rome. Although it was smashed to pieces long ago, the piece seen here is part of the 15 percent of the map that survives. It is enough to help archaeologists find their way around the ancient city.

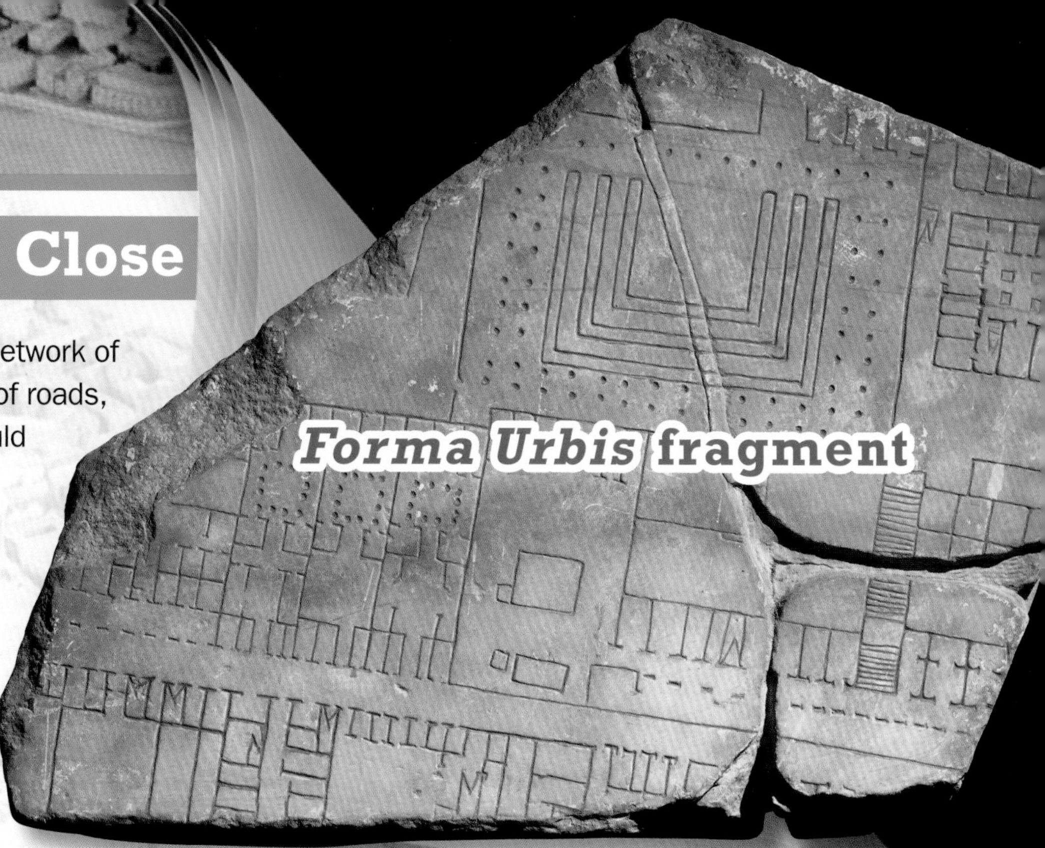

Forma Urbis fragment

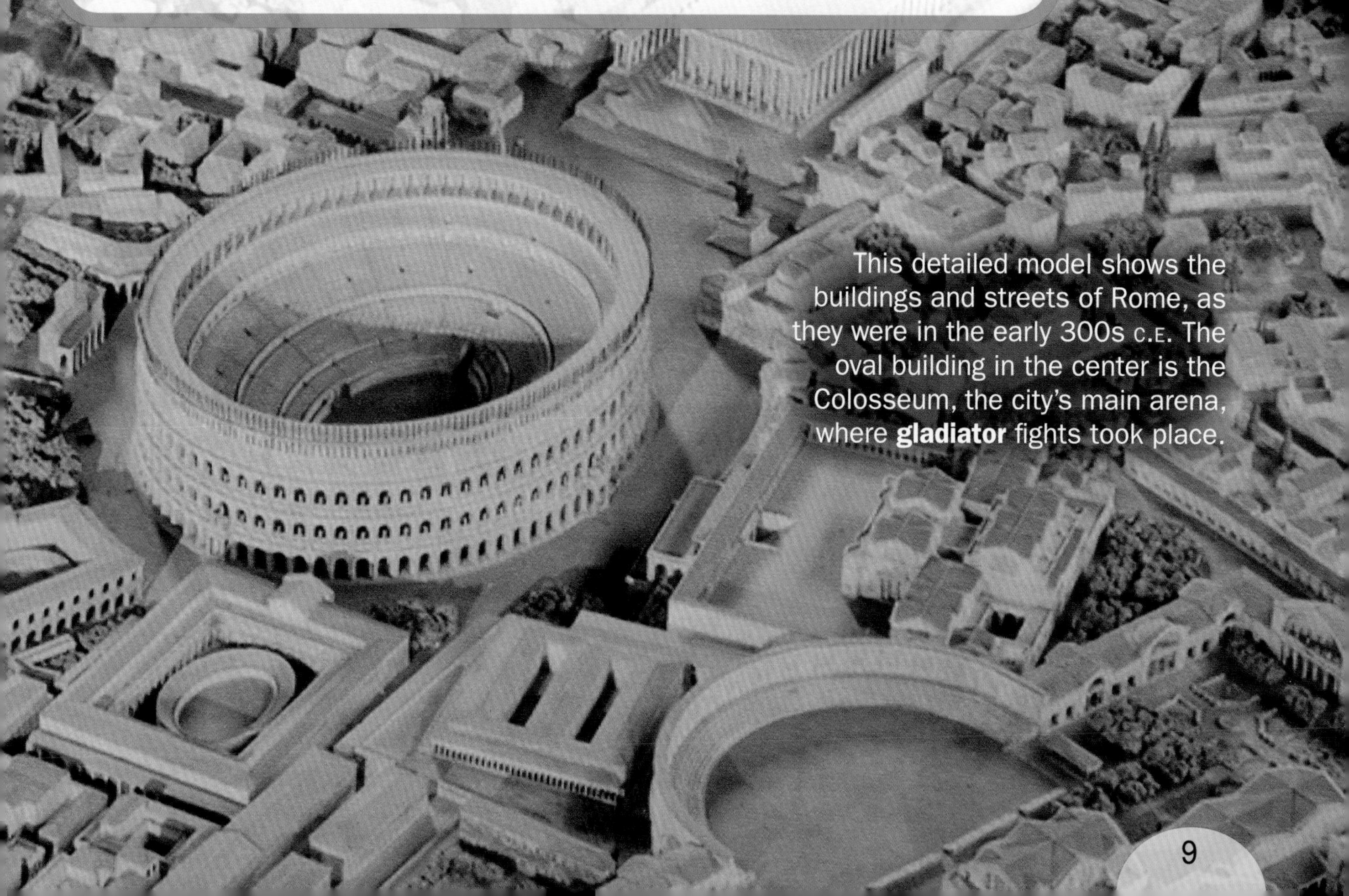

This detailed model shows the buildings and streets of Rome, as they were in the early 300s C.E. The oval building in the center is the Colosseum, the city's main arena, where **gladiator** fights took place.

9

A ROMAN FAMILY

To the Romans, a family meant a father, mother, their children, their sons' wives, their children, slaves, and the extended family clan, whether or not they lived under the same roof. Every member of the family knew their place, and took their responsibilities seriously.

Men and Women

The oldest living male was the head of the family, or "pater" in the Roman language. He expected the family to respect him and obey his word. His job was to provide for the family, educate the children, and offer prayers to the household gods who protected the family. He set a good example for his sons to follow. Women looked after the home, caring for the children, making the family's clothes, shopping for food, and preparing meals. If the family had slaves, they would do much of this work around the house.

Children and Childhood

Children were named at a ceremony when they were a few days old. Prayers were said, and they were given a lucky charm, called a **bulla**, to wear. Boys from wealthy families went to school to learn **Latin** and Greek, arithmetic, history, and astronomy. Girls and children from poorer families did not go to school. Girls learned how to look after the family home, preparing them for adult life. Childhood ended for girls when they were about 14, and for boys when they were 16. They took off their lucky charms, and dressed and behaved as adults. They could then get married and start families of their own.

The small Roman town of Pompeii, in the south of Italy, was home to about 15,000 people. It was destroyed by a volcano in 79 C.E.

History Up Close

Roman men wore a garment called a **toga**. It was a large semicircle of plain, woolen cloth, which hung loosely from the shoulders down to the toes. A man wore his toga over a **tunic**, and usually needed someone to help him drape it around his body to make sure all its folds were in the right places. This marble statue shows an important Roman man, possibly an emperor. We can tell this because his toga is very carefully folded.

statue of a Roman man in a toga

11

ROMAN TECHNOLOGY

The Roman Empire depended on engineers. They built roads that linked the empire as it grew. They also developed a new type of building material that made it possible to build bigger, stronger, and more **elaborate** buildings.

Roman Roads

Towns across the Roman Empire were connected by a network of good-quality roads. Many were built by Roman soldiers, allowing the army to travel quickly across new territory. In time, merchants and other travelers used the roads, and more places were connected to the network. In total, about 50,000 miles (80,000 km) of stone-paved roads were built.

Concrete

The hard-wearing building material that we call concrete was first used by the Romans in the 200s B.C.E. It completely changed the construction industry. Roman concrete was made from tiny pieces of crushed rock, tile, or brick, mixed with gritty, ashy sand, lime, and water. It was mixed into a stiff paste, then poured into wooden molds or around wooden frames. As it dried, it set hard.

Aqueducts

Roman towns needed large amounts of clean, fresh water for public drinking fountains, baths, and toilets. Much of the water was supplied by **aqueducts**, which were channels built with gentle slopes that allowed water to flow downhill. They brought water into towns from rivers, lakes, and springs. The city of Rome had 19 aqueducts. They filled huge tanks with water. From there, a network of pipes carried the water around the city.

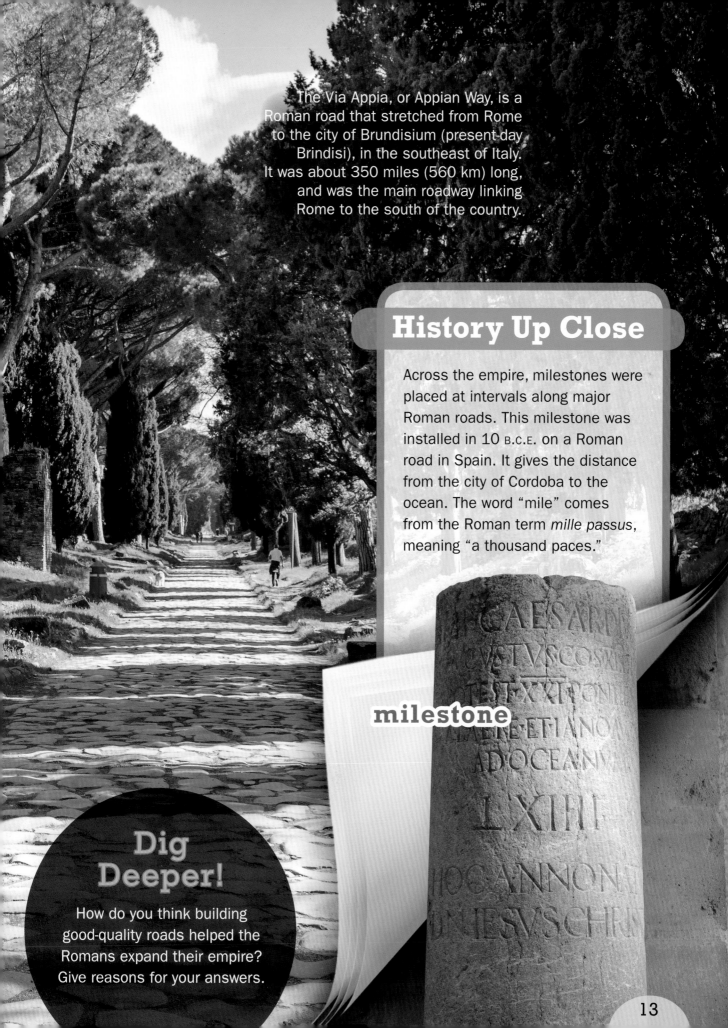

The Via Appia, or Appian Way, is a Roman road that stretched from Rome to the city of Brundisium (present-day Brindisi), in the southeast of Italy. It was about 350 miles (560 km) long, and was the main roadway linking Rome to the south of the country.

History Up Close

Across the empire, milestones were placed at intervals along major Roman roads. This milestone was installed in 10 B.C.E. on a Roman road in Spain. It gives the distance from the city of Cordoba to the ocean. The word "mile" comes from the Roman term *mille passus*, meaning "a thousand paces."

milestone

Dig Deeper!

How do you think building good-quality roads helped the Romans expand their empire? Give reasons for your answers.

FARMING AND FOOD

Farming was an essential part of Roman society. In the countryside around Roman towns in Italy, farmers grew crops, raised animals, and made wine and olive oil. They produced the food that fed the population.

Landscape and Crops

Large areas of Italy are covered by mountains, so Roman farms were located mainly in lowland areas. The main crop was wheat, which was ground into flour for making bread. Farmers also grew barley, oats, beans, and lentils, as well as vegetables such as cabbages, onions, garlic, and lettuce. The warmer climate of southern Italy was good for growing fruit, especially melons, plums, figs, apples, and pears. Farmers grew olives for eating, as well as for their valuable oil. Grapes were grown throughout Italy. Some were eaten fresh, but most were made into wine. Farmers kept sheep, cows, and goats for milk and meat. They also raised pigs, hens, geese, and pigeons, and raised bees for their honey.

Food on the Table

Poorer Romans had one meal a day, served in the evening. It was a basic meal of bread, grain porridge, cheese, and vegetables, with water or wine. In contrast, meals for the rich could be feasts that lasted late into the night. They enjoyed fish, snails, birds, meat, vegetables, fruit, nuts, and pastries—with plenty of wine.

Today, farmers in Italy grow their crops in the lowland parts of the country, just as their Roman ancestors did.

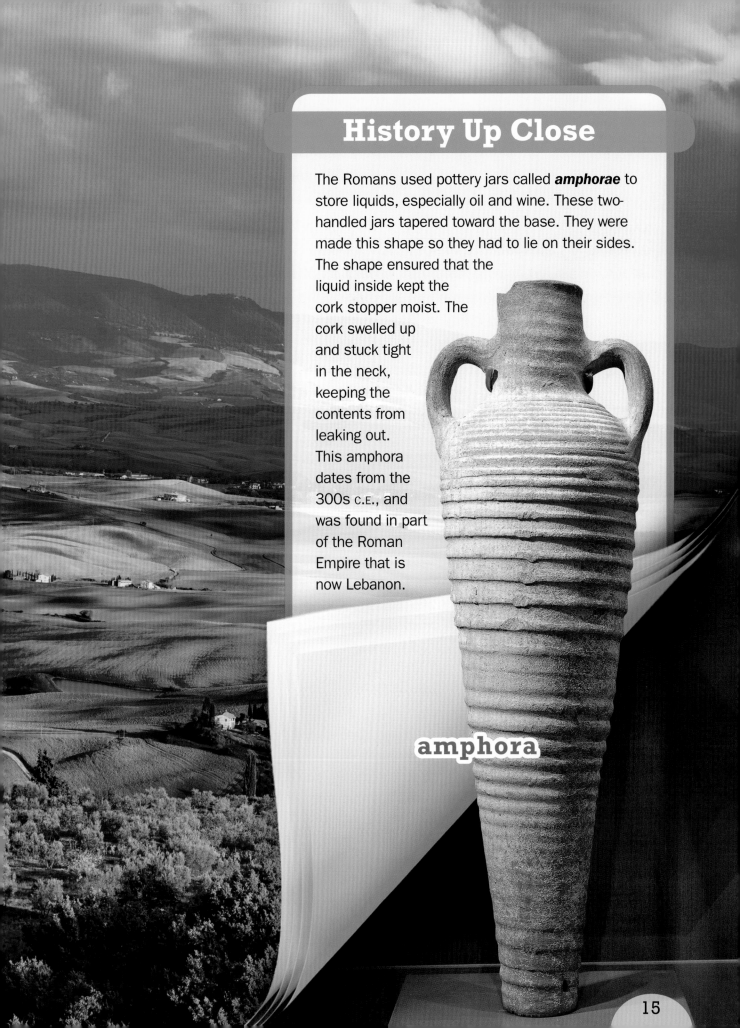

History Up Close

The Romans used pottery jars called **amphorae** to store liquids, especially oil and wine. These two-handled jars tapered toward the base. They were made this shape so they had to lie on their sides. The shape ensured that the liquid inside kept the cork stopper moist. The cork swelled up and stuck tight in the neck, keeping the contents from leaking out. This amphora dates from the 300s C.E., and was found in part of the Roman Empire that is now Lebanon.

amphora

ROMAN ENTERTAINMENT

The Romans celebrated a lot of festivals and holidays. Most were religious, but others marked state events such as when a government official took office. On festival days, people enjoyed themselves. They might watch a play, cheer chariots racing, or watch gladiators fight.

A Day at the Races

A town's *circus*, or racetrack, was the place to watch chariots race around a long, oval track. The chariots had two wheels, and were pulled along by teams of two or four horses. Charioteers belonged to four teams, named after the colors they wore (the Whites, Reds, Greens, and Blues). The biggest racetrack was the Circus Maximus, or Greatest Circus, in Rome, where chariots raced seven times around the track at speeds of up to 47 miles (75 km) per hour. The charioteers needed great skill to control their horses and avoid crashing into the other chariots.

Animal Hunts and Gladiator Fights

The most impressive entertainment was at the **amphitheater**—a large, open-air building. The largest of all amphitheaters was the Colosseum in Rome, where 50,000 people watched animal hunts in the morning and gladiator contests in the afternoon. Gladiators were trained fighters, and there were many different types. The *retiarius*, or net fighter, moved quickly, trying to catch his opponent in his net. He was usually matched against a *secutor*, or chaser, who wore armor and carried a shield and short sword. If both men fought well, the crowd might let them live, but a man who fought poorly would hear the crowd call out "*Iugula,*" or "kill him!"

The Colosseum in Rome opened to the public in 80 C.E. Spectators sat on rows of marble seats, where the sloping sections are in this photograph. On hot days, a canopy was stretched across the top, providing shade to the spectators.

History Up Close

For protection, some gladiators wore metal body armor and fabric wrapped around their arms, but others wore none. It all depended on what type of gladiator he was. Many gladiator helmets have been found, such as this one (right), worn by a *secutor* gladiator. It protected his head, neck, face, and throat.

gladiator helmet

Dig Deeper!

Bronze armor was strong, but it was heavy and bulky. Do you think that would have caused a gladiator any problems? Why? Give reasons for your answer.

TEMPLES AND GODS

Roman religion grew from an ancient belief in spirits, or mysterious forces that controlled and guided people's lives. Over time, the spirits became gods, each with a name and special powers. Some gods were worshiped in only a few places. Other gods were known and worshiped throughout the Roman world.

Top Gods and Goddesses

The Romans had dozens of gods and goddesses. The most well known were adopted from the ancient Greeks or people the Romans **conquered**. The Roman god Jupiter, the king of the gods, was known as Zeus to the Greeks. The goddess Juno, known as Hera to the Greeks, was the wife of Jupiter. The ancient Romans believed war and conquering were important, so Mars, the god of war, was second only to Jupiter. People prayed and honored many different gods. There were gods and goddesses for wine, wisdom, livestock, love, volcanoes, and even keys and doorways.

Houses and Gifts for the Gods

The Romans believed that temples were the houses where the gods lived on Earth. Inside a temple was a statue of a god that contained that god's spirit. The statue faced out into the courtyard, where people left gifts on an **altar**. Their gifts could be anything from a few crumbs of bread to a sheep or a goat. In return for their gifts, people hoped the gods would protect and help them. The greatest temple was the Pantheon. It was built in Rome between 118 and 125 C.E. Unlike other temples, which were for single gods, the Pantheon was for all the Roman gods. As sunlight came through an opening in the roof, it lit up the inside of the temple to reveal the statues of gods.

The soaring dome of the Pantheon is 141 feet (43 m) high.

statue of Mars

History Up Close

Mars was the Roman god of war. At the start of a military campaign, Roman soldiers called on Mars to help them. They cried out "Mars *vigila!*" which means "Mars, awake!" This marble statue of Mars was made about 100 C.E., and was found in Rome. It shows Mars as a soldier, with helmet, metal breastplate, and knee-length leather skirt with overlapping metal plates. In his hand, he holds a spear.

19

THE ROMAN ARMY

The Roman army was a powerful fighting force. Its job was to defeat Rome's enemies and protect the Roman Empire. Roman soldiers were highly trained, and their fighting methods and weapons brought them many victories.

Organizing the Army

The Roman army was at its greatest strength in the 100s C.E., when it had about 150,000 soldiers. It was divided into **legions**, each of which had about 5,500 men. Most of these were foot soldiers called **legionaries**. There were also a small number of **cavalry** soldiers within each legion. Each legion was divided into 10 **cohorts** and within a cohort, soldiers were put into groups called centuries. A **century** had 80 men in it (at one time it was 100 men) and was led by a **centurion**. Above the centurion were six officers called tribunes, who advised the legion's commanding officer, the **legate**.

Weapons and Armor

Roman soldiers carried special equipment and wore specific battle uniforms. A legionary was given a dagger (*pugio*), a short sword (***gladius***), and a heavy **javelin** (*pilum*). Soldiers wore strips of flexible metal and leather armor and a metal helmet, and carried a large, rectangular shield. While on the march, legionaries each had to carry an extra 90 pounds (40 kg) of equipment on their back for making camp. In battle, the army also used heavy weapons such as **catapults**. These machines could fire arrows tipped with iron, or hurl rocks over long distances to batter down an enemy's defenses.

The ruins of the Roman fort of Vindolanda, built in northern Britain in around 85 C.E. Many of the Roman soldiers stationed there were far from home. They came from the Roman province of Gaul, which is in present-day France.

testudo formation

History Up Close

Trajan's Column was built to celebrate Emperor Trajan's victory against the tribes of Dacia, a territory in present-day Romania. It was built in Rome about 110 C.E. Its carvings teach us a lot about the Roman army and its battle tactics. One scene shows a formation known as the *testudo*, or tortoise. A group of legionaries hold their shields above their heads. The shields protected them from arrows and stones, just like the shell of a tortoise.

EMPEROR AND STATE

For 500 years, the Roman Empire was ruled by emperors. Augustus was the first emperor in 27 B.C.E., and Romulus Augustulus, a 16-year-old boy, was the last, in 476 C.E. In total, the Roman Empire was ruled by about 80 emperors.

Running the Empire

The emperor was the leader of the Roman Empire, and it was his duty to control and protect it. That was a difficult task because the empire was so large and it contained so many different groups. To make it easier to control, the empire was divided into territories called provinces. Each province was ruled by a governor, who was the emperor's representative. It was the governor's job to collect taxes and make sure that Roman laws were obeyed. The governor was expected to protect the province. He could use the army to fight off attackers and deal with rebellions.

Good and Bad

Some emperors were good and were loved by the people. Marcus Aurelius, who reigned from 161 to 180 C.E., was thought of as the perfect emperor. He was devoted to his duties of looking after the empire. Others were disliked and feared. Emperor Caligula, who reigned from 37 to 41 C.E., was considered a terrible emperor. He had many people killed, and wasted money on things such as keeping his favorite horse in an expensive marble stable. He was killed by his own soldiers.

bust of Emperor Hadrian

Hadrian's Wall is 73 miles (117 km) long and was built in the 120s C.E. during the reign of Emperor Hadrian. It runs coast to coast across northern Britain and marked the northern boundary of the Roman Empire. The stone and turf wall had large forts and small fortlets or milecastles along its route, where Roman soldiers were stationed.

History Up Close

Hadrian, who reigned for 21 years (117–138 C.E.), was one of Rome's greatest emperors. We know what he looked like because many marble **busts** of him have survived, such as this one probably carved during his reign, and found in Athens, Greece. Hadrian was the first Roman emperor to grow a beard, and he started a fashion that was followed by many emperors who came after him. He visited Britain, which was Rome's most northerly province, in 122 C.E. and ordered a boundary wall to be built, known today as Hadrian's Wall.

CRAFTS AND TRADE

Merchants and traders traveled to Rome from all parts of the empire. Some came along the network of roads, while others came by merchant ship. They docked at the city's nearby port of Ostia, at the mouth of the Tiber River.

Made by Hand

Craftworkers made everything by hand, from the cheapest pottery bowl to the most expensive gold jewelry. Animal hides were turned into leather for shoes, boots, and sandals. Blacksmiths heated iron in **forges**, until it was red hot and soft enough to be beaten into shape. Painters decorated the walls of houses with patterns and scenes, while sculptors created beautiful statues from marble. Weavers produced cloth, glassmakers made glass vessels and windows, and jewelers worked with gold and silver to make earrings, necklaces, and bracelets.

Trade Across the Empire

The most important **commodity** traded by the Romans was wheat, which arrived by ship from Roman provinces in North Africa. It was used to make bread to feed the people. In Rome, the authorities gave free bread to the poor. They worried that riots might break out if they became too hungry. Wool, hides, tin, and wild animals came from Rome's province of Britain. **Papyrus**, a type of writing paper, came from Egypt. Wine came from Spain, France, and Greece, and olive oil was brought from Spain and North Africa. Some luxury goods came from beyond the empire, such as silk from China, jewels from India, spices and perfumes from Asia, and amber from the Baltic region to the north.

The Romans decorated floors and walls with **mosaics**. These artworks used tiny squares of colored stone to make detailed pictures. This tree mosaic was made during the 300s C.E. and was found in Paphos, Cyprus, an island in the eastern Mediterranean.

History Up Close

Olive oil was burned in clay lamps, like this one which was made in the 400s C.E. Oil lamps, some with decorative patterns, were made in workshops throughout Italy. A wick in the spout was dipped into the oil. The wick soaked up the oil, and a small flame burned at the end of it. The top of the lamp was slightly bowl-shaped, and when it needed filling up, oil was poured into the bowl, and dripped through holes into the lamp.

oil lamp

LEGACY OF ANCIENT ROME

Even though the civilization of the Romans ended about 1,500 years ago, the modern world owes a lot to the Romans. They left behind a great legacy, which continues to influence us to this day.

Words and Numbers

Latin, which was the language of the Romans, is no longer spoken as an everyday language, but modern Italian, French, Spanish, Portuguese, and Romanian are all based on it. Even the English language has many words that are based on Latin words. Most of the letters in our alphabet come from the Roman alphabet, and the names of all 12 months have Roman links. For example, August is named after Augustus, the first emperor. The Romans gave the names of their gods to the planets Jupiter, Venus, Mars, Mercury, and Saturn. Roman numerals are still used on clocks, and follow the names of rulers such as King Henry VIII.

Law and Government

In Roman law courts, cases were tried by a judge and jury—a system that is widely used today. Many countries have legal systems based on Roman law, especially those in Europe and North America. Like Rome was in its early days, many countries are republics today, including France and the United States. The government of the United States is organized in a similar way to the Roman Republic, with a Senate, Assembly (House of Representatives), and Consul (president).

Trajan's Market, in Rome, was a large market complex with five levels of stores and offices. It was built from concrete and red brick between 100 C.E. and 112 C.E.

Capitoline wolf

History Up Close

The Roman founding myth about the twin boys Romulus and Remus, and how they were fed by a she-wolf (see page 6), has inspired artists throughout the ages. This famous bronze statue of the wolf and the twins is a symbol of the city of Rome. It is displayed in the city's Capitoline Museum. It has long been known that the figures of the twins were made in the 1400s, and added to an older statue of a wolf. The question is, when was the wolf made? For many years, historians thought it was ancient, and was made in the 400s B.C.E. Recent tests revealed it was made around 1100 C.E.—a long time after the Romans! It is a good example of how modern science can be used to help us to correctly understand the past.

Dig Deeper!

What do you think was the greatest contribution made to civilization by the Romans: roads, their use of concrete, their engineering feats, or their legal system? Where can you see these contributions in your daily life? Give reasons for your answers.

MAKE A ROMAN LAMP

Oil lamps were the most common ways to light buildings in the ancient world. Most homes had several small clay lamps that could easily be carried around. Olive oil was commonly used as fuel. The first lamps were formed by hand. Over time, they were mass-produced using molds. These artifacts can reveal a lot of information. The type of clay used can indicate where a lamp was created. Many lamps were marked by their makers with a stamp or signature.

Using Molds to Make Lamps

The Romans mass-produced lamps by using a two-part mold system. First, wet clay was pressed into each half of the mold. Then the two halves were joined together and left to dry a little. Next, the molds were removed. The Romans then used a sharp tool to make a hole in the lamp for the oil and wick. Finally, the lamp was fired in a special oven called a kiln for around two days, until it was completely set and dry.

This terra-cotta Roman lamp was made using a mold, which allowed the detailed design on top to be easily reproduced.

Activity:

Make a Roman Lamp

Make a Roman lamp in two ways—by hand and with a mold.

You Will Need:

- Newspaper
- Air-drying clay
- A long strip of cotton
- Scissors
- Olive oil
- Small plastic bowl
- Plastic wrap
- Knitting needle or utility knife

Safety note: Do not light your lamp. This activity must be completed with adult supervision.

Instructions

1. Cover your work surface with a layer of newspaper.
2. Work the clay with your hands. Form a lamp shape that will not leak.
3. With adult supervision, use a knitting needle or utility knife to make openings for the spout and to fill the lamp. Allow the clay to fully dry.
4. Cut the cotton into three strips. Braid them together to make a wick. With adult supervision, fill the lamp with a small amount of olive oil.
5. With adult supervision, feed the wick through the spout using the needle or knife. Make sure the wick is soaked in olive oil. Trim any excess off the wick with the scissors so that it sits just inside the spout.

The Challenge

Make a second lamp using a plastic bowl as a mold. Line the bowl with plastic wrap, then press in clay to form one half of the lamp. It should be 1–2 inches (2.5–5 cm) thick. Allow the clay to dry a bit, then carefully remove it from the bowl. Follow the same steps to make a second piece that is the same shape. Join the two pieces together, then use extra clay to close the seam. Make holes for the oil and wick, and use extra clay to form a spout. Let it dry.

Why do you think the Romans started to use molds to make lamps? What are some advantages of using a mold to make items such as lamps? What are some disadvantages?

step 2

spout

step 4

wick

step 6

GLOSSARY

Note: Some bold-faced words are defined where they appear in the text.

abdicated Gave up one's throne

altar A flat-topped block used to make an offering to a god

amphitheater Open-air building used for shows, such as gladiator contests

amphora Large pots for storing wine, oil, or sauce; The word *amphora* means "two-handled"

analyze To examine

archaeologists People who study the past through the materials people left behind

artifacts Objects made by humans that give information about a culture or historical way of life

aqueducts Human-made channels for carrying water from one place to another

busts Statues showing only the head and shoulders of people

catapults Weapons that launch missiles through the air

cavalry Soldiers on horseback

centurion Commander of a company (century) of legionaries

century Company of 80–100 soldiers

circus A racetrack for horse-drawn chariots

citizens Originally refered to men born in Rome to Roman parents; Eventually, people across the Roman Empire were granted the right to call themselves citizens

cohorts Units of 480 soldiers in a legion

commodity A good that is bought or sold

conquered To have overcome and taken control of something

crisis A time of great difficulty, trouble, or danger

elaborate Containing a lot of careful detail

emperor The ruler of the Roman Empire

empire All the provinces ruled by the Romans, or the time when Rome was ruled by emperors

forges Workshops where metal is heated and shaped

gladiator A highly trained fighter, named after his main weapon, the *gladius*

gladius Short sword used by a gladiator

interpret To figure out the meaning

javelin A long spear-like weapon that is thrown

Latin The language of the Romans

legions Divisions of 5,000 to 6,000 soldiers

marble A hard-wearing stone used for buildings and statues

mosaics Pictures usually made of small colored stone squares

noble Someone with a high social rank that they have inherited from their parents

overthrew Used force to remove from power

papyrus A type of paper made from the flattened reeds of the papyrus plant

political Relating to the government of a country

primary sources Raw materials, such as tools or written documents, created during a specific period of time

republic State or country governed by officials elected by the people

rival Competing for the same object or goal

surveyors People who examine land and buildings, and divide up land

testudo A formation of soldiers; it means "tortoise" because they locked their shields over their heads to form a protective shell

tunic A knee-length garment, similar to a long shirt

Learning More

Want to learn more about ancient Rome? Check out these resources.

Books

Deckker, Zilah. *Ancient Rome: Archaeolology Unlocks the Secrets of Rome's Past*. National Geographic Children's Books, 2007.

Dickmann, Nancy. *Ancient Rome*. Capstone Press, 2016.

Doeden, Matt. *Tools and Treasures from Ancient Rome*. Lerner, 2014.

James, Simon. *Ancient Rome*. DK Children, 2015.

Johnson, Robin. *Understanding Roman Myths*. Crabtree Publishing, 2012.

Mehta-Jones, Shilpa. *Life in Ancient Rome*. Crabtree Publishing, 2005.

O'Shei, Tim. *Secrets of Pompeii: Buried City of Ancient Rome*. Capstone Press, 2015.

Waldron, Melanie. *Geography Matters in Ancient Rome*. Heinemann-Raintree, 2015.

Websites

Learn about 10 innovations from ancient Rome from History.com.
www.history.com/news/history-lists/10-innovations-that-built-ancient-rome

Explore Emperor Trajan's column and the story of his victories in the war in this interactive article from National Geographic.
www.nationalgeographic.com/trajan-column/index.html

National Geographic presents a list of articles about ancient Rome.
http://nationalgeographic.org/education/ancient-rome

Find out about gladiators and their bloody battles at this site from PBS.
www.pbs.org/empires/romans/empire/gladiators.html

Visit ancient Rome and learn about some of its most remarkable buildings in this video.
https://smarthistory.org/ancient-rome

INDEX

ABOUT THE AUTHOR

John Malam studied Ancient History and Archaeology at the University of Birmingham, England. He has written many information books for children, particularly on ancient civilizations.